"In this exquisite chamber piece about trauma, intimacy, and terror, Erin Courtney brings her inimitable sweet-savage vision to an exploration of the mystery of human consciousness. How do we understand who we are, and who we are to each other? How do we make sense of the fractures that trauma cracks into our minds? The underexplored overlap between science and theology, objectivity and love comes to life in this funny, heartstopping gem of a play."

—Madeleine George

"'I am a scientist,' declare two of the protagonists of the deliciously titled *Ann, Fran, and Mary Ann*. And Ann and Mary Ann are scientists, married to each other. Fran is a tile artist. Then there's a third scientist girding this play. It is the writer Erin Courtney—a true scientist of poetics and drama—giving us life-force language, firm form, and rounded, clear edges to create the play as vessel, a vessel as magical and secure as a lab beaker which holds the shaky beauty of these three women and the moment in time when they cross paths. Erin puts questions of God, effects of trauma, distrust in our bodies, and brain science under her singular microscope and creates a page-turning play that feels utterly of this moment and then tethered to a kind of forever. 'Listen to me,' Ann and Mary Ann implore each other finally. Let's listen to and through them because Erin chose to find these characters and this story—and because it's like a fact that we should as often as possible listen and look to Erin Courtney as one of our guides to the feelings we hold inside and outside ourselves."

—Tina Satter

53 SP 34
February 2021
Brooklyn, NY

Ann, Fran, and Mary Ann
© Erin Courtney 2021
53rdstatepress.org

Ann, Fran, and Mary Ann is made possible by the New York State Council on the Arts with the support of Governor Andrew M. Cuomo and the New York State Legislature.

Book design: Kate Kremer

ISBN Number: 978-1732545205
Library of Congress Number: 2020948313

Printed in the United States of America

ann, fran, & mary ann

by Erin Courtney

53rd State Press
Brooklyn, NY

contents

Introduction by Sarah Lunnie   7

Ann, Fran, and Mary Ann   14

Breathing in patterns: a conversation   113

introduction

"Pattern is so powerful. It can create a feeling of safety, for sure, but it can also create a feeling of anxiety. That's why I take design so seriously because the patterns that I create are going to take up residence in someone's home or someone's office and my pattern is going to invade their psyche."

—Fran, *Ann, Fran, and Mary Ann*

"Rose is a rose is a rose is a rose."

—Gertrude Stein, "Sacred Emily"

When Erin Courtney visited the literary office at Playwrights Horizons to tell Adam Greenfield and me about her commission-in-progress, she brought a visual aid. "Can I show you how I want the play to work?" she asked.

Reaching into her bag, she produced four cardboard squares, Xeroxed patterns pasted on their faces. We didn't know what we were looking at.

✦

When we'd been sheltering in our apartment for about a week, my husband competed in a virtual crossword puzzle tournament from our kitchen table while I, seven months pregnant, laughed at him from our couch. It was March; we were making the best of it.

In August, I sit at the same table trying to write while he and our infant son sleep in our bedroom. The world is falling apart. My brain doesn't want to make sentences. Again and again, I pull out my phone. I'm reaching not for the crossword—my brain doesn't want to make words, either—but for Tiles, a "soothing matching game," which the Times app assures me "may help me de-stress," and with which I have become fixated in our confinement.

One tileset I like is called "Holland." It features a lot of pastel-colored tulips. I'm supposed to tap two tiles with a matching feature—a green leaf shooting up on the right side of a stem; a blue bud drooping down on the left—to "remove the shared element." I keep doing this until I clear the board, the pattern becoming less and less coherent, eventually reduced to a boneyard of contextless parts, and finally nothing. Then I reset the board and start again.

Other tilesets—"Hong Kong," "Lisbon," "Kuala Lumpur"—are less representational, accumulating patterns through abstract geometrical shapes. These are even more satisfying to deconstruct. Sometimes my husband and I wonder aloud why this stupid game is so compelling. I think of Erin and her paper tiles.

In the office that day at Playwrights Horizons—it feels like another lifetime, or planet, but was in fact 2017—Erin demonstrated how, when you rotate the identical tiles in arbitrary directions and place them in a line, their parts don't accumulate into a coherent image. The effect is disjointed and chaotic. But if you change the relationship of these parts to one another—say, by stacking the tiles two by two to form a larger square, and rotating them so they mirror each other across an access—a new, unifying pattern emerges.

The image's constituent parts, when replicated and brought into harmony, generate a sense of order and balance.

If you rotate one of the tiles and disrupt the reflection, the order is disturbed.

This is how our brains experience the world, Erin explained. That is to say, associatively, looking for patterns. When we find them, we feel whole. When we can't, we feel broken, out of control.

"This is how I want my play to work."

Tomorrow is October. Last night, on national television, the President of the United States sowed doubts about the legitimacy of the upcoming election, refusing to commit in principle to a peaceful transfer of power. Last week in Kentucky, a grand jury failed to charge for her death any of the white police officers who shot and killed 26-year-old Breonna Taylor while she slept in her bed. California and Oregon are on fire. All the theaters are closed; who knows when they will be able to open. Around the world, more than one million people have died from COVID-19. My infant son is sleeping in the next room, he is cutting his first baby tooth, and my brain doesn't want to make sentences. I can't find the pattern.

It's hard to write about trauma while the world is falling apart. I go back to dismembering tiny digital tulips.

꩜

Ann and Mary Ann are married.

Ann and Mary Ann are neuroscientists.

Ann and Mary Ann both witnessed violent murders when they were children.

Ann's patient, Fran, believes her husband has been kidnapped and replaced with an imposter. This possibility, though terrifying, might be easier than reality for Fran's mind to accept.

Fran is a tile designer.

Mary Ann didn't believe in God, and then she did, and now . . .

Erin Courtney is not only a playwright, but also a visual artist; it does not surprise me that her imagination lit up as she learned about the brain science of trauma. Nor that she found a visual metaphor to assimilate the human truths she uncovered.

Nor that, in the crystalline play that she assembled from these insights, her words themselves function as objects, accumulating until they begin to bend.

The women in this play mirror one another, until they

don't. Each of them is attempting to survive in a world that contains such wild pain that her brain short-circuits at the fact of it.

How does chaos become incorporable?

It is humbling to think about this question in the middle of a storm.

Relief, Erin is showing me, doesn't come from avoidance or escape, but from repetition and rearrangement. You allow the truth to tessellate and fill the plane. You wait for it to become coherent.

You take it in until your mind learns how to hold it.

—Sarah Lunnie, September 2020

characters

ANN—Black, 40s-60s, female-identified or gender nonbinary, a cognitive neuroscientist and psychiatrist, married to Mary Ann.

MARY ANN—White, 40s-60s, female-identified or gender nonbinary, a theologist and neuroscientist, married to Ann.

FRAN—Latinx, 20s-40s, female-identified, a visual artist and tile designer.

note

When there is / in the text, it indicates an interruption, an overlapping of the dialogue. The following character speaks over the line.

setting

On stage, there are two almost identical labs.

Stage left is ANN'S LAB.

Stage right is MARY ANN'S LAB.

There is a wall between their labs with a door.

On the back wall of both labs is a large mirror.

If you look at it quickly, it looks like there are four labs on stage:

"Trauma almost invariably involves not being seen, not being mirrored, and not being taken into account."

—Bessel van der Kolk, M.D.

in mary ann's lab

Ann and Mary Ann sit in office swivel chairs.

They sit across from each other and look directly at each other.

They are both wearing lab coats.

Ann and Mary Ann are doing a Meisner-like mirroring exercise that their couples' therapist has assigned to them.

ANN
I am a scientist.

MARY ANN
I am a scientist.

ANN
I am a scientist.

MARY ANN
I am a scientist.

ANN
I am a scientist.

MARY ANN
I am a scientist.

ANN
I am Ann.

MARY ANN
I am Ann.

ANN
I am Ann.

MARY ANN
I am Ann.

ANN
I am Ann.

MARY ANN
I am Mary Ann.

ANN
I am Mary Ann.

MARY ANN
I am Mary Ann.

ANN
I am Mary Ann.

MARY ANN
I am Mary Ann.

ANN
I am your wife.

MARY ANN
I am your wife.

ANN
I am your wife.

MARY ANN
I am your wife.

ANN
I am your wife.

MARY ANN
I am your wife.

ANN
I am your wife.

MARY ANN
I saw God.

Slight pause.

ANN
I saw God.

MARY ANN
I saw God.

ANN
I saw God.

MARY ANN
I saw God.

ANN
I am not what you see.

MARY ANN
I am not what you see.

ANN
I am not what you see.

MARY ANN
I am not what you see.

ANN
You see you.

MARY ANN
You see you.

ANN
You see you.

MARY ANN
You see you.

ANN
You see you.

> *To the audience, brisk and presentational in tone:*

ANN
I am a cognitive neuroscientist and I am a psychiatrist and I am married to Mary Ann. My name is Ann.

MARY ANN
I am a neuroscientist and a theologist. I am married to Ann. My name is Mary Ann.

ANN
Let's go back to the start.

> *Ann and Mary Ann both breathe in for five counts and breath out for seven counts.*
>
> *Ann and Mary Ann both breathe in for five counts and breath out for seven counts.*
>
> *Ann and Mary Ann both breathe in for five counts and breath out for seven counts.*

ANN
Both Mary Ann and I witnessed murders
when we were very young.

MARY ANN

I was six and I saw my mother murdered by my father.
The murder I witnessed began with a thin knife that
cut right through my mother's neck.
My mother's movements were stopped by my father.
That is why the two hemispheres in my brain
have a hard time communicating with each other.

ANN

I was four when I saw my father killed by a police
officer. My mom, dad, and I were coming home from
the grocery store.
At the store, my parents bought cauliflower.
I had never heard the word cauliflower before so
in the back seat of the car, I was repeating the word
cauliflower,
turning the sounds of the word over in my brain,
when I saw my father shot.
My reaction to the trauma was dissociation, a leaving
of the body, a going blank.

MARY ANN

Both Ann and I were "subjects" in a Post Traumatic
Stress Disorder study in college.
In the study, they had us recount the murders in vivid
detail.
They wrote it down and called it a trauma script.

ANN

They had us listen to our trauma script over and over and over again as they scanned our brains. It was incredibly stressful. Our bodies each time believing it was happening now.

MARY ANN

But we were both science nerds, so we endured it, because we wanted to understand it and we hoped the study would help others.

ANN

And we hoped the study would help ourselves.
One attribute of subjects with severe PTSD is that they rarely make direct eye contact.
When the study ended,
I looked up
and I made eye contact with Mary Ann.
I saw Mary Ann.

MARY ANN
And I saw Ann.
And that is how we met.

> *There is the sound of something breaking in Ann's lab.*
>
> *Mary Ann opens the door between the labs to see.*

There is a person in Ann's lab.

in ann's lab

> *Mary Ann enters Ann's lab.*

> *Mary Ann is surprised to see Fran waiting there.*

> *Mary Ann and Fran make eye contact.*

MARY ANN
Oh! I didn't know you were here. You must be Fran.

FRAN
I am Fran.

MARY ANN
Nice to meet you. I'm Mary Ann.
How did you get into Ann's lab?

FRAN
Her assistant let me in.

MARY ANN
Can I get you anything?
Coffee? A water?

FRAN
No. Thank you.

MARY ANN
Did James give you a form?
Yes? Go ahead and fill that out and Ann will be right
with you.

Mary Ann leaves. Fran stares at the form.

in mary ann's lab

MARY ANN
Fran's here!

ANN
Now? She's early.

MARY ANN
James let her in and then left.

ANN
James!

MARY ANN
He gave her the induction form.

To audience:

I thought we had more time.
Okay, I will move this along.
Three years ago,
I saw God.

And.
The fact that I saw God
almost broke up our marriage.
You see,
when Ann and I got married,
we were both agnostic.

ANN
Atheist!

MARY ANN
I was agnostic, Ann was—is—an atheist.

But then, three years ago, I was demolishing our rotted-out deck in our backyard and under one section of the deck I found a dead bird. Just the body. The head had been ripped off. It was a beautiful red bird with no head. Later, in another part of the yard, I found the bird's head! Also red. A tuft of yellow on the top. A little perfect bird's head next to our back fence.

I was regarding this decapitation when suddenly every color in the yard became so bright and everything was surrounded by light and I could see all of the molecules around me vibrating and there was no boundary between me, the ground, the air, the leaves.

I felt this unity with everything and I felt safe and I felt loved.

And I knew this was God.

I was in the presence of God!

I was, immediately, changed.

I was different.
Ann did not believe it was God.
We are both scientists, so we argued for quite some time about what it could be, it went like this:

ANN
(To Mary Ann) You had a seizure in your left temporal lobe.

MARY ANN
(To Ann) I knew you were going to say that.

ANN
Because that is clearly what it was!

MARY ANN
It was not a seizure, Ann.
I'm going to prove it to you.

To audience:

Before I saw God, my main area of study was sleep, the brain and sleep.
But after I saw God
I quit my original study and began to study how the brain and spirituality intersect.

ANN
She built. A God Helmet.

MARY ANN
A Trans-cranial Magnetic Stimulator.

ANN
A God Helmet.

MARY ANN
Fine.
A God Helmet.
It stimulates, with tiny electromagnetic pulses,
the temporal lobes of your brain.

Mary Ann puts the God Helmet on Ann.

MARY ANN
I will turn the motor on. If you feel any uncomfortable
sensations or if you hear a ringing sound in your ears,
hold up one finger and I will turn it off. Practice holding up one finger.

Ann holds up one finger.

Mary Ann turns the motor on.

Ann feels the magnetic pulse.

Ann's face changes slightly.

MARY ANN
What are you feeling?

ANN

I feel good.

MARY ANN

Good. Good. Do you see anything?

ANN

Oh! It felt like I was blind for a moment.
Everything went dark.
Oh. Oh
I can see a bit now.
I am starting to recover.
I am in a forest filled with heavy vines.
The vines are everywhere, blocking the path.
I need to rewire them.
Not rewire them.
I thought they were wires for a minute but no, they are
vines, I just need to move them.
What are my neurons doing?

MARY ANN

Ann, stay focused on what you see, not what you think
your brain is doing.

ANN

Oh, the sun is streaming through the vines now.
Wow!
There is a revolution of light.
Beautiful streaks of light!
Oh I see two eyes looking back at me.

It's a troll!
A little old troll is peeking at me from behind a giant tree.

> *Ann reaches her hand out in front of her.*
>
> *She is trying to touch the troll.*
>
> *Mary Ann is disappointed and a little bit angry.*
>
> *Mary Ann takes the helmet off Ann.*

MARY ANN
(To audience) What Ann saw should not have surprised me.
Some people experience a feeling of oneness with the universe,
some people experience a spiritual awakening,
some people have intense, detailed memories,
and some people see something supernatural.
Ann saw something in the supernatural category.
That should not have bothered me.
But it did bother me.
It also bothered me to realize that I had hoped—expected?—hoped
that she would see or feel
God.
Because after that day in the backyard, everything changed for me.
I didn't just "see" the world differently.
I felt it differently.

I felt all this love, all around me.
And for the first time in my life, I felt safe.
I felt no fear.
I had never in my life
experienced
a true absence of fear.
I wanted Ann to feel that.

ANN
(To Mary Ann) I don't want to believe in God.

MARY ANN
It's not God that I want for you.

ANN
Then what is it?

MARY ANN
I want you to feel safe. Let's try again. Please?

ANN
Fine. Because I love you very much.
And because I want you to stop bothering me about it.
And because I love you.

MARY ANN
Thank you!

> *Ann puts the helmet back on.*
>
> *Mary Ann turns a dial.*

MARY ANN
What do you see?

Ann is smiling a little.

She is reaching out for something we can't see.

ANN
Oh my God.

MARY ANN
What is it?

ANN
It's my living room with the orange carpet.
It's the house on Cushing Drive!
I see my dad.
He's smiling.
And he's holding something.
One little pink striped sock
and one little purple polka-dotted sock
He is making the socks do a little dance.
Like Charlie Chaplin
with the potatoes on the forks
in that movie.
He's singing a little song
about lucky socks. Lucky socks.
He's laughing. Lucky socks.

Ann is laughing.

Mary Ann turns off the helmet and takes it off.

Ann looks down at her two brightly colored, mismatched socks.

ANN
I call my socks
lucky socks
I didn't know that I got that from him.

MARY ANN
(To audience) Ann was so happy to have recovered that memory of her dad.

ANN
(To audience) The God Helmet brought me my Dad!
So I stopped making fun of the God Helmet.

MARY ANN
(To audience) And Ann did her work and I did my work and everything was great until Fran arrived.

in ann's lab

Ann enters her lab.

ANN
Hi Fran. I'm Ann.
Let's get started.

Did you complete the form?

FRAN
Yes.

ANN
Great. Can I get you a coffee or a glass of water?

FRAN
Water would be great, thanks.

> *Ann gets Fran a glass of water.*

> *Ann is looking at Fran's answers on the questionnaire.*

ANN
I see that you answered that you are not claustrophobic.

FRAN
I actually love being in small spaces. It makes me feel safe.

ANN
That will be very helpful for our work because some people do become claustrophobic in the MRI machine and if that happens we can stop the scan immediately. Okay. And I see here that you design tiles for a living?

FRAN
I do!

ANN

What a wonderful job! I love tiles. I love patterns!

FRAN

Me too!

ANN

In another life, I would have liked to have been an artist.

FRAN

In another life, I would have liked to have been a neuroscientist.
All the books next to my bed are popular science books.

> *Ann looks back down at the form that Fran filled out.*

> *Ann can't read Fran's writing.*

ANN

And your husband's first name is Banker?

FRAN

Barker.

ANN

I bet he got teased a lot as a kid.

FRAN

He did. Bark! Bark! Bark!

ANN

Before this event with Barker, have you ever experienced a trauma?

FRAN

My whole life, I never experienced a trauma.

ANN

A trauma, such as a car accident, death of a loved one, illness, divorce, abuse?

FRAN

I had the most ordinary childhood.
I went to school.
Did my homework.
Ate my broccoli.
Ate my cauliflower.

> *Ann has some strange reaction to the word cauliflower.*
>
> *Ann leaves the room without apology or explanation.*
>
> *Fran waits. Ann returns.*

ANN

Have you ever experienced depression? Anxiety?

FRAN

None! I remember telling my friends that I don't have a dark side.

I am great at communicating, staying in touch with friends and family.

I never took anti-depressants.

I had friends that suffered from depression

and I saw how their brain chemicals were causing them so much pain.

ANN

Have you ever had any trouble staying organized, forgetting words, or a feeling of disorientation?

FRAN

I don't know what it is about my brain but it has always worked really effectively!

I don't know if it is all this work that I do with geometry and art, but it seems to me that

my two hemispheres of my brain have always worked in perfect harmony.

People say you have a more dominant left brain or right brain but I feel like I have a really good balance.

I am visual and creative but I also stay organized and use logic to keep my mind from spiraling into negative thinking.

ANN

How about stress in your career?

FRAN

I am successful in my career.

ANN

So tell me about why you are here today. What happened?

FRAN

You already know what happened. Everyone knows.

ANN

It's important that you tell me in your own words.

FRAN

I was out of town at a convention. I hate to do these design conventions but I have to do them to get new clients. They are extremely boring and at the same time exhausting. I'm bone tired and I get this call on my cell phone from a private number, and I let it go to voicemail. A few seconds later, it rings again and now I am thinking, oh no, I have a bad feeling. I have a feeling this could be something bad.
And it was something bad.
It was Barker and he was at the police station and he was under arrest.

ANN

What did he tell you?

FRAN

He told me that there had been an accident.
He told me that he had shot a man in self defense.
Barker said that the man was an intruder,
that the intruder was moving strangely
and that he had a gun.

ANN

Did the man have a gun?

FRAN

No.

ANN

How old was the man?

FRAN

He was a teenager.
Fourteen years old.

ANN

What time of day was it?

FRAN

3:30. In the afternoon.

ANN

Where did the shooting occur?

FRAN

On our doorstep.

You saw it on the news.
Everyone saw it on the news.
Our neighborhood has surveillance cameras
so it was recorded
and everyone saw what happened.

ANN

I need for you to tell me what happened.

FRAN

The kid was an exchange student.
He was staying with a family in our neighborhood and
he had gotten lost.
He didn't speak a lot of English.
He was carrying a backpack
and he took something out of his backpack.
Barker saw a gun.

ANN

What did Barker say on the phone to you?

FRAN

Barker tells me that the man he shot is dead and that
he is in jail and that I need to come home right away.
He says it was self defense and I need to get him out
of jail. So I get the first flight. And CNN already has
the footage and they keep showing it over and over, on
a loop, and I keep watching. I am sitting in the middle
seat with strangers on either side of me and I just keep
watching. Our house. Our front door. This lost kid, his

face in a shadow. Barker opening the door. The kid looking for something in his backpack. And then a shot and then the kid falls down onto our cement walkway and Barker closes the door. First of all, I was against having a gun in the house. I have always been against guns in general and guns at our home in particular. But part of being married is learning which battles to fight. The gun made Barker feel safe. I let him keep it, because he kept it locked up, and he felt safer having it in the house. And I keep watching the video over and over and over. It was self defense, he told me. But the police didn't find a—the teenager didn't have a gun. I keep watching the video and I am feeling sick to my stomach. Barker shoots and he closes the door.

Pause.

I get to the visiting area at the jail. I am so scared to see Barker because I don't know what I will feel when I see him and they take me to see him and when I do see him, I am so confused and relieved at the same time because I can see that this is NOT Barker. He looks exactly like Barker, like a duplicate copy, but I know my husband and I know this is NOT my husband. This was an imposter posing as Barker. An exact double.

ANN
How did you know he was an imposter?

FRAN

He was a stranger.

A stranger that looked exactly like Barker.

ANN

Okay. What happened next?

FRAN

I try to listen to what he is saying
but I know he is an imposter.
I know he is not my husband.
Finally, I can't stand to pretend anymore
so I start asking him,
Who are you? Who are you?
and then yelling at him
Where did you take my husband?
Why did you do this?
and I am screaming.
They take me to the psych ward, and after a lot of
interviews, a lot of these same questions
over and over until they decided I was not a threat to
myself or others, they released me into my brother's
care and they told me I should come talk to you, and
my brother made me promise to at least come and talk
to you. You don't think I am crazy do you?

ANN

No. I don't. I have seen this before. This has happened
before.

FRAN

I knew it had to be a pattern. That there must be a reason that someone took my husband. No one else believes me. No one is helping me.

ANN

I am going to help you.

in ann's lab

The next day.

Ann is trying to work. She is typing notes into her laptop.

Mary Ann is on a break from her work. She holds a 5"x 8" cardboard card about a foot away from her face.

She stares intensely at a black dot on the cardboard card.

She moves the card slowly towards her nose.

MARY ANN

I can't find my blind spot.
I am following all the directions!
I close my right eye.
I hold the card a foot away from my face.

I focus my left eye on that black dot.
I move the card slowly towards me, always keeping my eye on the black dot.

Mary Ann moves the card slowly to her face.

I can still see it.
Ann, grade school kids can do this!
Why can't I do this?

ANN

You're moving the card too fast. You have to move it more slowly.

Mary Ann tries again, moving the card slowly towards her face.

MARY ANN

I think it is because I have seen the thing that is supposed to disappear and so when I sense it entering into my blind spot, I adjust my left eye imperceptibly in order to "see" it.

ANN

Well. That's cheating.

MARY ANN

I know. But I don't want it to disappear.

ANN

That's why you can't tell the subjects of your study too

much about the experiment because they will want to control the outcome.

MARY ANN
It's scary to watch something disappear. Stop typing so loudly.

ANN
I am typing the volume that I always type at.

MARY ANN
You are pounding on the keys.
You're doing it on purpose.

ANN
I am not doing it on purpose. Put in your ear plugs.

MARY ANN
I lost my ear plugs.

ANN
But they are on your keychain.

MARY ANN
I lost my keys!

ANN
I'll help you look for them.

MARY ANN

No! I don't need you to help me look for them! I need
you to stop typing so loudly.

ANN

Why are you even in here? You have work to do, go
back to your lab and stop bothering me.

MARY ANN

Uh. Well. I want to talk to you about something.

Deep breath in.

Having Fran in your lab is—making me nervous—
It is making me feel really uncomfortable and.
I think you should refer her to someone else.

This suggestion makes Ann furious.

*Ann takes a moment to calm down before she
speaks.*

ANN

You know how rare it is to find subjects that have Capgras Syndrome!

MARY ANN

I know that. Of course I know that! I'm afraid she is
going to trigger you.
She watched her husband murder a kid!
Don't you think that is going to be a problem for you?

ANN

I can compartmentalize.

MARY ANN

I would feel a lot better if you had someone else in the room with you when you work with her.

ANN

James will be there.

MARY ANN

James is useless!

I'm serious.

We have both worked very hard to be healthy and to stay healthy.

We have to be vigilant.

ANN

Mary Ann. I hear you.

I know there's a risk that Fran's story could trigger me.

I will keep track of my behavior.

Okay?

If I forget words, lose time, get disoriented, dissociate.

I will tell you.

Deal?

MARY ANN

You have to tell me!

ANN

I promise to tell you.
I need Fran in order to publish.
If I don't publish, I don't get tenure.
If I don't get tenure, we don't have a lab.
We don't have a lab then we can't work.

MARY ANN

Okay. I love you. I love you and I worry.

ANN

I love you too.
I love that you worry.

> *A nice moment of connection.*

> *Ann moves a piece of hair off of Mary Ann's face, or she kisses her hands.*

> *Mary Ann smiles and does something silly.*

> *Some little physical in-joke, a signal that all is well.*

> *Ann really sees Mary Ann.*

ANN

How's your work? Any new subjects coming in?

MARY ANN

Yes! Next week, I have a mystic coming to try out the helmet.

ANN

A mystic?

MARY ANN

He's clairvoyant and he sees things and often the things that he sees come true.

ANN

(Suspicious) What kind of things?

MARY ANN

He saw his mother's kitchen on fire and he saw her hands in flames. That evening she called him from the hospital, she had been making a meal and the grease caught fire and she suffered third-degree burns on both hands.

ANN

Uh huh. Have you ever had a self-proclaimed mystic in the helmet before?

MARY ANN

Ann. Sometimes when I tell you about my work I can feel your disdain. It's like you try to bury it deep in the folds of your psyche but it just comes out.

ANN

I do not feel disdain for your work. I am a good person.
I support you.

MARY ANN

What script is that? Did you memorize that for when
you feel trapped by me?

ANN

I don't feel trapped by you. I was being sincere!

MARY ANN

Okay. That's a ghost of an old argument.
I know you don't think this is "real science" but it is.
It is "real science" and you don't need to believe in God
to understand the relevance of this work.

ANN

Of course!
I just—
A mystic? Mary Ann?

MARY ANN

I know. I know.
I know your work is the reason we are here.
I know the University doesn't take my study seriously,
but I want *you* to take it seriously.

in ann's lab

Ann is at work in her lab.

Fran is pacing in a state of high excitement, still wearing her coat and holding her purse.

FRAN

I heard from Barker!
He's alive! Oh, Ann, he's alive!
I spoke to him on the phone, but, well it was confusing because—
SHIT—
I don't know how to explain it.

ANN

Okay. Let's take it one step at a time.
Have a seat, Fran.
Take off your coat, stay awhile, ha ha.

Fran takes off her coat and purse.

FRAN

The phone rang and the caller ID said it was the county jail so I wasn't even going to pick up because I thought, why is the imposter calling me? I don't want to speak to him!
But something compelled me to answer the phone. And I am so glad that I did!

Fran is near tears.

It was Barker on the phone! It was him.
I was so happy.
"You're alive! Barker! You're alive!"
And my heart was so full, hearing his voice—
And I was like,
"Where are you?"
and he says he is in the county jail.
"No! The imposter is in the jail! Not you."
And Barker tells me, there is no double,
he IS in jail
it was self defense
and that I have to testify
as a character witness.
BUT
I figured it out.
Barker is being held captive somewhere.
The imposter has an accomplice and the accomplice
has Barker.
The accomplice has a way of patching the phone call to
LOOK LIKE it is coming from the jail.
The accomplice is telling Barker what to say.
They want me to believe that Barker is the one in
the jail cell so that I will give up looking for the real
Barker.
At least I know he is alive, Ann.
Barker is alive and when I heard his voice I just felt
so full.

He said "I love you."
He's alive.

> *Ann holds up a large photo of a white man.*

ANN
Is this Barker?

> *Fran studies the photo.*

FRAN
No. That's the imposter.

in mary ann's lab

> *The next day, Ann and Mary Ann are eating their lunches out of tupperware.*

MARY ANN
So why does she recognize him as the real Barker when they talk on the phone but not in the photograph?

ANN
Think about it. Rev up that motor in your mind. You got this.

MARY ANN
Oh, right, the auditory link to memory is not damaged at all.

ANN

Bingo. As long as she isn't looking at him, she has access to her feelings and memories and she can recognize him as him, because she feels something.

MARY ANN

That must be so confusing for her.

ANN

Yeah. Her brain is working so hard to explain this phenomenon.

MARY ANN

It's eerie. The way everything is working in her brain except this one thing. This one, really big thing.

Silence.

Did you do the shopping this morning?
I want to make that NY Times cauliflower recipe.

ANN

I parked in the Whole Foods parking lot.

MARY ANN

Uh huh.

ANN

And I had the list in my hand.
And I could not get out of the car.

*Ann pulls the list out of her pocket and looks
at it.*

ANN
I'm sorry.

MARY ANN
Hey, that happens sometimes.

ANN
But it hasn't happened in years. I should be able to buy
fucking cauliflower!
I could not get out of the car.

Ann looks at herself in the mirror.

Ann looks worried.

*Ann continues to stare at herself in the mirror
for a long time.*

ANN
I really hate this mirror!

MARY ANN
It does make the lab look bigger.

ANN
I hate seeing myself all day long.

Mary Ann joins in the staring into the mirror.

MARY ANN

I know, I hate seeing myself too.
Ugh.

ANN

Can we please get rid of it?

MARY ANN

Actually, I have a contractor coming to give us a bid
on how much it would cost to remove it and re-plaster
the wall.

ANN

You do?

MARY ANN

Yeah. I was gonna surprise you.

ANN

Oh, you ruined the surprise!
I'm glad I know.
It's something to look forward to.
Thank you.

MARY ANN

It's funny, when we rented the lab, we both thought
that mirror would not bother us—

> *They both stare at themselves in the mirror.*

> *There is a sense of dread in the room.*

They stare for too long.

in ann's lab

Ann and Mary Ann, carrying to-go coffee cups, enter the lab.

Fran is already there, sitting and sketching in her notebook.

ANN
Oh! Fran! You're early.

FRAN
It's hard to be at home.

ANN
I understand.

FRAN
My brother follows me from room to room with this really worried look on his face.
I don't know what he thinks is going to happen to me, that my head is going to explode?
He just looks so worried.
I just needed to be in a different space.
I hope you don't mind.
I was just working on some new designs.
It helps calm me down.

ANN

No. That's great!

FRAN

I was thinking about your lab here—
You could put a tile mural up there.
I could design one for you.

MARY ANN

That's so funny, because we do want to get rid of that
mirror!

FRAN

When I was a little girl. I would just stare and stare at
any tile pattern I came across.

I would rearrange them in my mind and try to figure
out how to construct the opposing image. Flip, rotate,
flip, repeat.

Pattern is so powerful, it can create a feeling of safety,
for sure, but it can also create a feeling of anxiety. That's
why I take design so seriously because the patterns that
I create are going to take up residence in someone's
home or someone's office and my pattern is going to
invade their psyche. It's as though my design is trespassing on your life.

You see my pattern while you brush your teeth or as
you walk down the hallway to your office.

I was looking at this mirror and this room and I began
sketching four hemispheres.

And I was thinking of this set of four as one cluster.
Each hemisphere reflecting and rotating the shapes of
the design
and at first it was just abstract shapes
and then I began to make associations and
the shapes began to suggest an image
and the image was a hummingbird,
well, two hummingbirds.
See?

MARY ANN
OH MY GOD! I LOVE HUMMINGBIRDS.

ANN
She does! We have like ten hummingbird feeders outside our kitchen window.

MARY ANN
How did you know that?

FRAN
I don't know! I just started drawing it.

MARY ANN
That's amazing.

> *Ann gets a text on her phone.*

> *Ann whispers to Mary Ann.*

ANN

James is sick!

MARY ANN

What?

ANN

James just texted in sick. Fran. Will you excuse us for
a moment?

FRAN

Of course.

Mary Ann and Ann step into Mary Ann's lab.

ANN

I was going to work on Fran's trauma script today.

MARY ANN

I know.

ANN

Do you want me to cancel?

MARY ANN

Uh. No. No. I'll help you. If it's okay with Fran.

Ann and Mary Ann return.

ANN

Fran, for this part of the work I need an assistant. James
has called in sick and Mary Ann has offered to assist

me for today. May I have your permission to allow Mary
Ann to be present in the room?

FRAN

Of course.

ANN

I am going to ask you to recall very specific, sensory
details from the day you first watched the surveillance
footage of the shooting. After we have written the sensory details of that day, I will read it back to you while
you are in the scanner and we will see what parts of
your brain light up.

FRAN

Uhm. Why? Why do I need to recall details of THAT
day?

ANN

I understand that this is an uncomfortable memory and
I would not make you endure this if I didn't think it
would help.

FRAN

You think it will help find my husband?

ANN

I think it will give us information that will help you.
Yes. May I have your permission to record this conversation?

FRAN
Fine.

Fran signs a consent form.

ANN
Fran, I'd like you to breathe through your nose for five counts and then breathe out for seven counts. We will do that three times.

> *Ann, Fran, and Mary Ann breathe in for five counts and breath out for seven counts.*
>
> *Ann, Fran, and Mary Ann breathe in for five counts and breath out for seven counts.*
>
> *Ann, Fran, and Mary Ann breathe in for five counts and breath out for seven counts.*

ANN
Are you ready to begin?

Fran nods yes.

ANN
Let's begin with what you remember seeing when you sat down in the airplane seat.
What textures did you feel, what sounds did you hear, what did you smell?

FRAN

I remember the AC on the plane was up really high
and I only had a light shirt on. I was freezing cold
and they don't have blankets on the flights anymore. I
was moving my hands up and down my arms trying to
get rid of my goosebumps. I felt the seat belt and the
familiarity of buckling a seat belt. I was breathing really
fast. I was so worried about Barker and I turned on the
little TV in the seatback in front of me.

ANN

What did you smell?

FRAN

The woman by the window had a lot of perfume on.
And the man on the aisle was sweating and I could
smell his sweat. CNN was on the screen. They showed
the surveillance video. They showed our front door.
They showed the cement walkway. The branches of the
eucalyptus tree.
I don't see what this has to do with anything.

ANN

What do you remember touching as you watched the
video? What words were on the screen? What words did
the newscaster say?

FRAN

I don't remember!
I don't see how this will help you find my husband.

I need to use the restroom.

Fran leaves.

Mary Ann plays back the recording of Fran.

Mary Ann and Ann both type details into their laptops.

FRAN'S VOICE
I remember the AC on the plane was up really high and I only had a light shirt on. I was freezing cold and they don't have blankets on the flights anymore. I was moving my hands up and down my arms trying to get rid of my goosebumps. I felt the seat belt and the familiarity of buckling a seat belt.

There is a shift in the lab.

We go inside Ann's head.

Ann hears her own trauma script.

Mary Ann does not hear it.

ANN'S VOICE
I remember the upholstery in the back seat of our car. It was a brand-new station wagon and the back seat had a brown tweed fabric.
I remember rubbing my hand over and over the texture,

the little scratchy bumps and the smooth stripe of leather.
It was a really, really hot day.

So the little strip of leather was burning hot and even with the air conditioner on full blast, the inside of the car was hot. Everywhere was hot.

I remember my mom and dad in the front seat.
and I hear my mom say "I'm gonna bake the cauliflower with lots of cheese and then Ann will want to eat it."
and I tried to picture flowers baked in cheese
because I thought cauliflower was a type of flower
and I thought that would taste bad even with the cheese
I heard a siren. Really loud behind me.

I hear my mom say, "Slow down. You have to pull over"
I hear my dad say, "Damn it."
I hear my mom say, "You have to pull over."
I felt the car jerk to a stop. My dad muttering something.
I saw a police officer walk by my window.
I heard him tap on my dad's window.
I heard the sound of my dad's window going down.
The new car had electric window openers and they made a sound, and the window moved fast.
I heard the officer say, "License and registration."
I see my dad shift his body in order to reach the glove compartment.
My dad's leg was in a cast and his cast hit the electric window opener on his side
and his window starts to roll up and I hear the officer say,

"Don't roll up the window. Don't roll up the window.
Don't roll up the window!"
and then next thing I hear is gunshots
and my mom is screaming,
and my dad is bleeding.
and I am, I am . . .

> *There is the sound of a door slamming in the
> hallway.*
>
> *Ann jumps and has a look of terror on her face.*
>
> *Mary Ann looks shocked.*
>
> *Fran reenters the lab.*
>
> *Fran is angry.*

FRAN
I have to go.
My brother locked himself out of the house. I need to
let him in.
Ann! Ann, did you hear me?

ANN
Oh. Sorry. Could you repeat that?

FRAN
My brother is locked out.
I need to go meet him at my house.

ANN

Oh. Okay. We can continue this tomorrow.

> *Fran musters the courage to ask this question.*
> *She is furious.*

FRAN

Why are you making me remember watching that video?
How is that going to help me find my husband?

ANN

I need those details so I can watch what happens inside
your brain when you hear the details read back to you.

FRAN

But why THOSE details? THOSE details have nothing
to do with finding the people who kidnapped my husband and replaced him with an imposter.

> *Ann rubs her face. She is having a hard time*
> *coming up with an answer.*

FRAN

You said you have seen this before.

ANN

I have.

FRAN

You have seen a person replaced with another identical
person?

Pause.

You have seen a person replaced with another identical person? Answer me!

ANN
No. I have seen people who believe that to be true.

FRAN
You never believed me?
You lied to me!
Why did you lie to me?

MARY ANN
Let's all calm down.

FRAN
This is the most frightening experience of my life and you can look me in the face and tell me that it is beneficial for me to be lied to by you. I thought you were going to help me! You are not helping me!

> *Fran runs out.*
>
> *Ann freaks out.*
>
> *Ann paces the lab.*
>
> *Ann goes into Mary Ann's lab.*
>
> *Mary Ann follows her.*

in mary ann's lab

Ann paces around in Mary Ann's lab.

ANN
No, no, no, no, no, no
NO! No!

MARY ANN
Is she in danger of hurting herself?

ANN
Let me call her brother.

> *Ann pulls out her cell phone and begins to search for Fran's brother's phone number.*

I can't even use my phone.
I don't know what I am doing.
I don't know.
Help me, Mary Ann.
I'm freaking out.

MARY ANN
Here, let me find the number.

ANN
No. I just need.
I need a moment.

They sit together quietly.

MARY ANN
Do you want to do the reflection exercise?

Ann nods.

Ann and Mary Ann look at each other

ANN
I am a failure.

MARY ANN
I am a failure.

ANN
I am a failure.

MARY ANN
I am a failure.

ANN
I am a failure.

MARY ANN
I am a failure.

ANN
I want to help.

MARY ANN
I want to help.

ANN
I want to help.

MARY ANN
I want to help.

ANN
I feel like an imposter.

MARY ANN
I feel like an imposter.

ANN
I feel like an imposter.

MARY ANN
I feel like an imposter.

ANN
I left my body.

> *Slight pause.*
>
> *This is new information to Mary Ann.*
>
> *This is really bad.*
>
> *Mary Ann is frightened.*

MARY ANN
I left my body.

ANN
I left my body

MARY ANN
I left my body.

ANN
I left my body.

MARY ANN
I left my body.

ANN
This isn't helping! Stop! Stop.

MARY ANN
Breathing exercise?

ANN
No. No.
Can you put the helmet on me?

MARY ANN
Yes! Of course!

> *Mary Ann is delighted!*
>
> *Mary Ann puts the God Helmet on Ann.*
>
> *Mary Ann turns on the electromagnetic pulse.*
>
> *Ann breathes.*

MARY ANN
What do you see?

ANN
I don't see anything.
I don't see anything.
I don't see anything.

in ann's lab

A few hours later.

Ann is working alone in her lab.

Mary Ann is working alone in her lab.

Fran arrives.

ANN
Fran! I am so glad you came back!

FRAN
I didn't know where else to go.

ANN
Are you okay?

Fran has a horrible look on her face.

FRAN

I walked up to my house.

And I see my brother's back.

He's sitting on the little bench in our front garden

and I call out to him

and he turns around

and it's not him.

It's not him.

It's another double.

They took my brother too.

I don't know where to go.

Please.

I don't want to be locked up again.

Please.

ANN

I won't lock you up. I know I can help you. It's good
you came back.

FRAN

My heart is breaking.

I don't know what to do.

ANN

I am so sorry, Fran. It's good you came back here.

> *Fran walks by the big mirror on the wall.*

> *Ann is standing in the doorway between the
> two labs.*

Ann's reflection is not visible to Fran.

Fran points at her own reflection in the mirror.

FRAN
Who is that?

ANN
What do you mean?

FRAN
Why is that woman looking in on us? She looks really
upset!

ANN
You don't recognize her?

FRAN
No. I always thought this was a mirror.

ANN
What do you mean?

FRAN
Well, it's a window!
Who works over in those labs?

ANN
Have a seat, Fran.

Ann walks Fran to a chair.

Fran sits down, facing away from the mirror.

Can I get you a coffee? Or a water?

FRAN
Um, coffee would be good. Yeah. Yeah. I could really use a coffee.

Ann goes into Mary Ann's lab.

in mary ann's lab

ANN
Fran doesn't recognize herself in the mirror.

MARY ANN
What?!

ANN
She no longer has access to memories linked to her own face.
Oh no. This is. This is. Bad!
The one study I read where the person couldn't recognize themselves in the mirror did not end well.

MARY ANN
Oh. Oh. Okay.

ANN

I am getting her a cup of coffee. Will you come in with
me?

MARY ANN
Of course.

ANN

I need you to keep her mind occupied.
Don't ask her anything about her life.
Oh God!
She also does not recognize her brother.
Keep her facing away from the mirror.
I want to keep her stress level as low as possible.
I am going to call Dr. Davis and see if he can give me
any advice.
Oh God. My hands are shaking.

MARY ANN
Give me the coffee.

in ann's lab

Mary Ann brings Fran the coffee.

MARY ANN
Hi Fran. Here's your coffee.

FRAN
Where's Ann?

MARY ANN
She had to make a call and she'll be right back.

FRAN
Oh, my stomach is in knots. I don't think I can drink this.
They took my brother away too. They took my brother.

Fran hands the coffee back to Mary Ann.

MARY ANN
I'm sorry Fran.
I know this is hard.

FRAN
Why would someone do this to me?
I always thought of myself as a good person.

MARY ANN
You are a good person.

FRAN
I don't understand who would want to take my family.

Fran gets up and paces.

Fran glances at the lady in the mirror.

FRAN
Why is she being studied?

MARY ANN
She is in a lot of pain. Fran, please sit.

FRAN
I don't know what to do.
I almost drove earlier
into a tree
en route here.
I wanted not to, shit, not to feel these feelings.

MARY ANN
Did Ann ever tell you about what I am studying?

FRAN
No.

MARY ANN
Would you like to hear about it?

FRAN
Okay.

MARY ANN
It's in the field of neuro-theology which means I am studying how spirituality and the brain intersect.

FRAN
Oh. I never heard of that.

MARY ANN
It's a relatively new field of study. And let me tell you,

if you had told me even three years ago that I would become anything with the word theology attached to it, I would have laughed you right out of the room. My grandmother was religious and she took me to church. I didn't mind it. But I didn't believe in it. I just had a sort of discontinuous relationship to the whole thing. My eye would study a stained glass window, then my eye would be drawn to the back of the pew, to the little shelf that held the prayer books, and I would say the words but I only thought of them as sounds, I didn't ponder the meaning, I just never really thought about God. It was just a series of movements. Kneel. Sit. Stand. Open book. Read along. Watch the dust motes in the stream of light coming through the window. But then three years ago, I had a spiritual experience in our yard. I saw God.

> *Fran has stopped listening and is hyperventilating.*

FRAN
I can't breathe. I can't breathe.

MARY ANN
Okay. Okay.

> *Mary Ann rests her hand on Fran's shoulder.*

Look at me.
Breathe in slowly.
Good.
Can I get you a glass of water?

Fran nods yes.

Mary Ann gets her a glass of water.

Fran drinks.

Fran breathes.

Can I tell you more about my work?

Fran nods yes.

MARY ANN
When I saw God, I was different. It's hard to explain, I
felt one with everything, I couldn't tell where I ended
and where everything else began.

FRAN
That sounds frightening.

MARY ANN
It wasn't.
It was—
It was beyond language.
But of course
I wanted to see what my brain was doing
and so I built a
God Helmet.

FRAN
A what?

MARY ANN

It's a helmet that stimulates your temporal lobe using tiny electrodes, tiny magnetic pulses.

FRAN

Does it hurt?

MARY ANN

Oh no. It's totally painless. I started collecting data on the brain activities of monks and rabbis and priests and atheists and agnostics. It's funny, I never thought of how religious people have trained their brain through lots of practice to achieve a transcendent state. I was sort of blind to the rigor that exists in theological communities. And even when atheists wear the helmet, they experience pleasant memories or have supernatural visions.

FRAN

People always see pleasant things? In the helmet?

MARY ANN

Yes! Happy memories. A feeling of wellness. I often see hummingbirds having sex.

Fran smiles!

MARY ANN

I know! I feel one with the universe and I see hummingbirds having sex. That's why your tile design surprised me so much!

A wave of panic washes over Fran.

FRAN
I'm so scared.

> *Fran begins to pace like a wild animal in a cage.*
>
> *Fran begins to touch objects in a strange way.*
>
> *Mary Ann is frightened.*
>
> *Fran opens the door to Mary Ann's lab.*
>
> *Fran enters Mary Ann's lab.*
>
> *Fran looks in the mirror and screams.*
>
> *Mary Ann jumps.*

FRAN
That woman is in here too!

> *Eager to calm Fran down, Mary Ann rushes after her.*

MARY ANN
Fran.
Fran.
Fran.
Please sit.

FRAN

Why would people, why would people want me to suffer, why are they taking away my family?

MARY ANN
Please sit, Fran.

FRAN
And no one is helping me!

MARY ANN
Fran.
Fran.
Fran.
Please sit.

FRAN
I just keep sighing and sighing. I can't stop sighing.
I don't know where my husband is. I don't know where my brother is.
I'm all alone.
I'm alone.

MARY ANN
I'm here with you, Fran.
Remember this is a safe place.
No one is hurting you here.
You are safe.
I am safe.

FRAN

Oh no, this is not, not safe at all.
I am not safe.
You are not safe.

MARY ANN
We are safe here.
We are safe here.

FRAN
I am not safe.
I need something.
I don't know what I need.

> *Fran again begins to pick up objects in a strange, threatening way.*

MARY ANN
Fran, please sit down.

> *Fran waving a heavy, dangerous object. She looks dangerous.*

FRAN
I have to do something.
I don't know what to do.

> *Fran yells into the mirror.*

Stop watching me! Go away!

Fran screams at her own reflection.

Time stops.

Mary Ann hears her own trauma script.

Fran doesn't hear it.

MARY ANN'S VOICE
I remember the stickers that I had put on my wall right
next to my bed.
When I heard them fighting, I would climb in my bed
and touch each of my stickers and count them.
First one by one, then by twos, then by threes, then
back to counting by ones again.
I remember I was counting by threes and I got to 33
and the scream in the kitchen was more horrible than
other screams I had heard
and I took the phone and I went under my bed and I
called 911
and I told them what I heard
and then it got quiet
and I went to go look
and my mom was sitting
at the kitchen table
very still
there were cereal bowls with cheerios in them
a lot of milk and just a few cheerios
and there was a plate
with a crust of toast

and the tea kettle was whistling
and my dad stood behind my mom
and he looked right into my eyes
and he drew the blade right across her throat.
and the tea kettle's screaming
and I was frozen

Fran has got her hands on the God Helmet.

FRAN
What is this?
Is this the God Helmet?

MARY ANN
What?

FRAN
This is the God Helmet? This?

MARY ANN
Yes. This is a God Helmet.

FRAN
I want to put this on.
I want to see God.
That will help me.
To see God.
Please. Put the helmet on me.

MARY ANN
No. I'm sorry.

FRAN

I need your help, now.

Please, I am in so much pain.

MARY ANN

I can't do that.

Fran is hyperventilating and pacing.

FRAN

Yes, you can!

I need this.

I need help.

Please help me.

Please, please, please.

MARY ANN

But you are not my subject. You are Ann's subject.

Mary Ann is frightened.

FRAN

No! I am not her subject anymore!

Please, let me find some peace.

Let me find some peace.

Please

Please

Please

help me.

Please.

I need to feel something good.

MARY ANN
It is a healing experience.

FRAN
Please!

MARY ANN
I wish I could, Fran.

FRAN
You can! You can!
Please.
My heart is exploding.
I've lost everyone and
I just need
I just need
a moment of peace
just a moment
away from this pain.
Please.

Mary Ann puts the helmet on Fran.

MARY ANN
I will turn the motor on. If you feel any uncomfortable sensations or if you hear a ringing sound in your ears, hold up one finger and I will turn it off. Practice holding up one finger.

Fran holds up one finger.

MARY ANN
Okay.

>*Mary Ann sits at the controls and turns on the electromagnetic pulse.*

MARY ANN
What do you see?

FRAN
I see. I see. I see a simple, gold ring, floating in darkness.
The light reflects off of it, piercing the darkness.
Now I see that I am outside an MRI machine, there is a light glowing inside of it.

MARY ANN
And now?

>*A sense of calm washes over Fran's face. Her body relaxes.*

FRAN
I see the Pacific Ocean.
Oh.
It's calm and bright.
Gentle.
Now the ocean is gone
and I am in my parents' bathroom,

looking at the old California tiles,
pink tiles with a black wave-like curl.

There is a change in Fran's face.

MARY ANN
What do you see now?

FRAN
I'm in the woods.
I see a transcendent spark.
The folds of the kindling are lit.
The fire is full and lighting up the sky.
Warming my hands.
The flames are making a pattern,
I am associating the flames
with ghosts and sleepwalkers.
I feel my soul.

Big inhale.

I feel my soul.

Big exhale.

It is flooding out into everything.
I feel like I can read the mind of everything.
I am a mystic.
Oh. All of that is gone now.
I am alone.
I am in isolation.

There is a fluorescent light.
There is an air of depression.
I look at the floor to see if the tiles have a pattern.
There are no tiles.
There is no pattern.
Wait. Oh! There's our front door.
It's Barker! In the door!
It's you!
It's really you!
Barker's pointing a gun -
Right at me.

Fran has a look of horror on her face.

He shoots me.
I am falling and I am bleeding on our walkway
I am
I am

Ann enters and is horrified to see Fran in the God Helmet.

She is in shock and is frozen for a minute.

I'm inside the body of the kid he shot.
I see Barker glance down at me.
Cold.
His face is cold.
He does not see me.
I am nothing to him.

I am nothing
and
I see him step back inside our house
and close the door.

ANN
Turn it off!
Mary. Ann.
Turn it off!

> *Mary Ann shamefully turns the electromagnetic pulse off.*
>
> *Mary Ann takes the helmet off of Fran.*
>
> *Fran is crying and crying and crying.*
>
> *Fran looks at herself in the mirror.*

FRAN
Oh God, my face is a mess.
I'll be right back.

> *Fran goes to the bathroom.*
>
> *There is a murderous silence.*

MARY ANN
She recognized herself in the mirror!

ANN
What did you do?

MARY ANN
She was suffering so much and I didn't want her to
suffer.

ANN
She is my subject!

MARY ANN
She was in so much pain.

ANN
It is the equivalent of murdering someone, / what you
did

MARY ANN
It is not the equivalent of murdering someone!
You can't say that to me!

ANN
I can say what I want to say!
I can say what I feel and
I feel fucking / betrayed by you.

MARY ANN
She recognizes herself again / in the mirror

ANN
You broke every rule that we have / as scientists. Why
do we have these rules if you are just going to smash
them?

MARY ANN
She needed my help.
She needed God's help.

ANN
God's help?

Fran reenters the lab.

She collects her things.

FRAN
I have to go.

ANN
Please stay. Tell me what happened.

FRAN
What happened?
That God Helmet fixed my brain.

Fran grabs the photo of Barker.

I see that this is my husband, Barker.
I know there is no double.
I know my brother will be at my house waiting for me.

MARY ANN
Please, sit down, this must be very traumatic.
Let us have your brother come get you.

FRAN
No.
No!
I came here because I wanted to find my husband.
I found him.
There he is!

Fran holds the photo of Barker!

This is the real Barker.
Right here.
In this photo.

Fran is shaking her head.

You know, my brother never liked Barker.
He never trusted him
and he told me,
just once,
before I married Barker,
he said-
"He's a time bomb."
my brother said.
He said-
He said-
"Fran, I'm worried you won't be safe with him-
You aren't seeing him clearly-"
and I said "If you believe that
about Barker,
you needn't come to our wedding."

He never mentioned it again.
He didn't want to lose me.
So.
He never said it again.
And he was right.
He saw something that I couldn't see.

Fran leaves.

Ann and Mary Ann sit there.

ANN
How could you do that?

MARY ANN
I don't know. I don't know what I was doing.

ANN
You knew exactly what you were doing.

MARY ANN
You said yourself,
you said it doesn't end well
when they can't
recognize themselves
in the mirror.

ANN
Why couldn't you wait five minutes for me to come
back here?

MARY ANN
I was trying to distract her.

ANN
Your God Helmet is not a distraction!

MARY ANN
I think I should get you a Xanax.

ANN
No.
I am wired and I should be wired.
You could have caused significant damage to her brain.
Your spiritual dysfunction has ruined everything.

MARY ANN
I helped her. You stopped seeing the human. The
human that's right there.

ANN
What you did was dangerous, / you were trespassing.

MARY ANN
That sensed presence of your dad, that helped you, that
reassured you, / I wanted her to feel some safety.

ANN
You took my work away from me.

A pause.

Why did you do it?

MARY ANN
She was in so much pain.

ANN
Why did you do it?

MARY ANN
I was in so much pain.

ANN
Why did you do it?

MARY ANN
She begged me.

ANN
Why did you do it?

MARY ANN
I was afraid she was going to hurt herself.
I was afraid I was going to hurt her.
I was afraid she was going to hurt me.
I was afraid I was going to hurt myself.
I lost God. I lost God. I lost God.

ANN
What?

MARY ANN

I know there is no God.
I am afraid all the time now.
As quickly as God arrived,
he left me.
Right after Fran got here,
the nightmares came back.
The feeling I had,
the belief I had,
was gone.
I haven't been sleeping at night, I've been seeing
my mother's eyes and
my father is holding the knife over my neck.
I can see her eyes in pain and
he's come back for me.
Come back to kill me.
And I tell my brain, this is only a dream.
And I force myself awake.
My heart is beating too fast
and I can hear the script of my mother's murder being
read to me through a microphone, there is a blinding
light, I am strapped down in the MRI machine, there
is a horrible piercing ring.
I just want it all to stop.
There is no God.
The feeling that I had
is gone.
It's gone.

I'm so scared.

A quiet moment.

Ann approaches Mary Ann slowly.

ANN
Losing God is not the problem.
This whole time you are ON ME about "You HAVE to
tell me if you have any symptoms!"
You made me promise to tell you and I did!
I told you everything—
about the fucking cauliflower
about leaving my body
and you didn't tell me anything.
YOU LIED TO ME!

MARY ANN
I didn't want it to be true.

ANN
You should have told me.

MARY ANN
I felt so safe
for three years
I was safe
I didn't want to admit
I wasn't safe anymore.

ANN
Admit it.
YOU GOT TO FEEL SAFE FOR THREE YEARS.
I never get to feel safe.
Never.
That's the reality.
That's the truth.

MARY ANN
I want you to feel safe.

> *Ann viciously stares into Mary Ann's eyes.*

> *They begin a dangerous version of the reflection exercise.*

ANN
I do not feel safe.

MARY ANN
I do not feel safe.

ANN
I do not feel safe.

MARY ANN
I do not feel safe.

ANN
I do not feel safe.

MARY ANN
I do not feel safe.

ANN
I do not feel safe.

MARY ANN
I do not feel safe.

ANN
I want to hurt you.

MARY ANN
I want to hurt you.

ANN
I want to hurt you.

MARY ANN
I want to hurt you.

ANN
I want to hurt you.

MARY ANN
I want to hurt you.

ANN
I want to hurt you.

MARY ANN
I want to hurt you.

ANN
I want to hurt you.

MARY ANN
God left me!

Silence.

God left me!

Silence.

God left me.

Silence.

God left me.

Silence.

God left me.

ANN
Listen to me.

MARY ANN
Listen to me.

ANN
Listen to me.

MARY ANN
Listen to me.

ANN
Listen to me.

MARY ANN
Listen to me.

ANN
Listen to me.

MARY ANN
Listen to me.

ANN
Listen to me.

MARY ANN
Forgive me.

>   *Silence.*

Forgive me.

>   *Silence.*

Forgive me.

>   *Silence.*

Forgive me.

ANN
See me, Mary Ann.

MARY ANN
See me, Mary Ann

ANN
See me, Mary Ann

MARY ANN
See me, Mary Ann.

ANN
See me, please.

MARY ANN
See me, please.

ANN
See me, please.

MARY ANN
See me, please.

ANN
See me!

MARY ANN
See me.

ANN
See me!

MARY ANN
See me.

ANN
See me.

MARY ANN
See me.

ANN
See!

> *Ann and Mary Ann stare out at the audience.*
>
> *They stare at the audience for quite a while.*
>
> *Fran enters the lab and joins Ann and Mary Ann.*

FRAN
(To audience) A few years after all this, I went to the Alhambra in Spain.
I stood under these arches and domes
and I breathed in all of the patterns,
all of the lines and circles and curves and grooves and stripes,
the tessellations
an impossible honeycomb

that soothed my mind,
a bath of repetition.
I began to feel whole again.
And I reached out to Ann and Mary Ann.
Would they like to study my brain now?

ANN
(To audience) I said to Fran:
We are not speaking to each other.
We are living separately.
We are working separately.

MARY ANN
Ann did not get tenure.
We lost that lab.
It was my fault.

FRAN
I said, well, it will probably never happen but.
but if you change your mind—
if you come back together—I want you, both of you, to
study my brain.
After all of this—
After all the trauma—
After the God Helmet—
What does my brain look like now?

ANN
She had to wait ten more years
but we came back together

and we found funding
to study how the brain can heal itself.

MARY ANN
About the impact of the trauma on her visual cortex, and
about how stimulating her left temporal lobe may have
reconnected the bridge between her perception and her
memory.

FRAN
I still have nightmares.
All the time.
Terrible nightmares of Barker shooting me.
Barker shooting that young man
over and over and over again.
It's a horrifying image.
It's a horrifying fact.
But I can see it.
I can see what is really truly right in front of me.
Oh! And I did design a tile mural for their new lab.
Here it is.

> *A beautiful, complex, unified tile pattern*
> *appears on the wall.*

It wasn't hummingbirds.
It's based on the architecture of the Alhambra.
If you haven't been, you need to go.
I was staring up at the carved ceiling
in the Hall of the Two Sisters

and I had an overwhelming urge to lie down
on the cold tile floor.
So I did.
I lay on the floor and
I relaxed my eyes so that I could try to see the entire
pattern all at once.
Could my eyes take in the whole swirling pattern all
at once?

> *Fran breaths in for five counts, exhales for seven*
> *counts.*

I was breathing in the air of centuries,
the ancient air of oppression and battles
and faith and art
and math and science.
I felt limitless.
And then I saw a tour guide peering over me.
"Ma'am,"
the guide says gently,
"Ma'am, you aren't allowed to lie down here.
Ma'am, please let me help you stand.
Ma'am, please stand.
Ma'am, please stand.
Please stand.
Please stand.
Please stand.
Please stand.
Please stand.

Please.
Please.
Please.
Please.
Please.
Stand."

Ann, Fran, and Mary Ann breathe in for five counts and breath out for seven counts.

Ann, Fran, and Mary Ann breathe in for five counts and breath out for seven counts.

Ann, Fran, and Mary Ann breathe in for five counts and breath out for seven counts.

THE END.

breathing in patterns

A conversation with playwright Erin Courtney, director José Zayas, and professor and psychiatrist Carl Erik Fisher.

Erin Courtney: José, it has been a real dream collaborating with you on this. You really embraced the rhythm of the play and you always returned to the way repetition is the heartbeat of the play. You also encouraged me to restore the ending that I had cut and I am so glad you did (spoiler alert). Can you talk to me about why you felt strongly the play needs to end the way that it does? What drew you to this play?

José Zayas: I'm an atheist but I grew up Catholic. Church every weekend, religion classes every weekday. And though I was surrounded by people who believed, I never did. I never questioned their right to believe and I hid my true feelings for most of my young life—mostly because I didn't want to upset my parents. I've never felt like I struggled with my lack of faith, though I wonder why I was able to see the world differently at such a young age. I wasn't taught this, it just was. I understood what I was being taught as metaphor, as story, as a way to shape the world around me and as a guide to figuring out how to treat people with empathy.

My early education left me with a deep appreciation for narratives that deal with the unknown, the unexplainable, the spiritual and the contradictory. I loved your play from the first page because it presented an immediate challenge and a mystery—it introduced me to neurotheology, it spoke in a language that I understood (the Meisner repetition exercise), but then made it "strange" by placing it in a new context. I "heard" these characters immediately but every time I read the play I discovered deeper layers of meaning and interpretation. In other words, it does what my favorite plays do best—it presents a problem and then it explores unrelated areas of expertise, giving us a broader view of the problem and a unique insight into a "solution." This does not mean that I expect a good play to solve a problem—that would be didactic and boring. A good play is emotionally messy, it presents possibilities and gives you the space to breathe and take from it what you need at that moment in your life. Narratives change depending on when you experience them and I love that this play actually makes this part of its form and that you as playwright have the craft to lure me in with a light touch while creating a dense tapestry of observation and thematic connections that leaves me shaken and delighted every time.

I also love that it is about three very intelligent and articulate women and that one of them is Latinx—I direct many plays that deal with the Latinx experience and identity and I am always excited to encounter a Latinx character who isn't defined solely by where they come from or what language they grew up with. Which is one of the reasons I wanted to hear Fran's voice in the ending. Your initial instinct was to let us hear her one more time but then you questioned it and thought that it might be better if the play ended at a moment of crisis and dissipation between Ann and Mary Ann—Fran never came back, the future was unknowable, the trauma was ultimately victorious. I love sad endings and I don't need a play to spell out its ending or give me false hope, but in this case it felt like it was an unfinished thought. I missed Fran saying "I breathed in all of the patterns" as a way to help me piece together the story that I had just seen—and I missed the three women breathing together at the end. They lead the audience in a shared breath before the lights dim. We know that people's hearts can literally beat together in a theater and I loved that the play can go from metaphor to actually landing on your body as a final gesture.

Carl, it's a pleasure to talk to you and I'm thrilled that we have all been brought together to share some thoughts about this lovely and prickly text. Over the years I've directed many plays that try to incorporate science into narrative to varying degrees of success. What makes a good science narrative in theater? What excites you as a scientist and what excites you as an audience member? And does this play use science in a way that is unique to theater?

Carl Erik Fisher: José, I resonate so much with what

you said about the need for messiness in plays. Science itself is messy, and I think it is wonderful and rare when art can reflect that messiness, not as something incidental to the "pure science," but as something deeply entangled with the very process of scientific investigation. There is a popular stereotype of science as "pure;" that the process of experimentation and investigation builds positively toward some pre-existing truth, brick by brick, adding knowledge to the scientific edifice. Sometimes this is how I see science portrayed in art in general. But nowhere is this antiseptic stereotype less true than in the case of research into human psychology, and especially human suffering. That's one of the things I love about this play. Even right from the very beginning in the character of Mary Ann, we meet someone who is both a theologist and a neuroscientist, and we know that the science in this play will not be some cold and abstract thing "outside" of humanity. I think it's far more interesting, if theater is to engage with science, to use theater as a way of probing and exploring how science is not separate from the rest of humanity, just as justice, history, faith, and belief are not separate.

Especially in psychology, researchers often study what has a personal resonance for them—trauma, anxiety, depression, whatever. I've heard this slandered as "me-search," a term that slyly suggests that someone's research is too biased by their own experience, as if a researcher with a history of depression should not be studying depression, for example. But this is unfair. Who doesn't have a personal experience of psychological suffering? Why pretend otherwise? I love how this play brings personal history in contact with science with such immediacy and urgency. Ann and Mary Ann met in the process of doing something arduous in an effort to help themselves and others. Later, questions about "help"—like who should help, and when to help, and how to help, and what is actually helpful?—become crucial to the action. I will attempt not to spoil the story or put my own narrow interpretation on it, aside from simply saying that the play invokes for me a key tension in clinical research. Medical researchers are doing the work to try to develop new ways of helping, but research is research (as opposed to simply practice) because we simply don't know that it will help. Subjects in psychiatric research, for example, have to sign long and detailed forms outlining how they may or may not actually benefit from the studies. And yet we are often doing it, scientists and "subjects" alike, because we hope it will help. A good word for that hope is faith, and I think it is a beautiful thing, and one that has to be protected with utmost care and respect.

Finally, I want to say that for me, the play invokes something important about the relationship of science to other social forces. Where we put the focus of scientific study matters a great deal; it is not a value-neutral decision, for example, to study trauma in terms of individual biology versus psychology versus the way generations of systematic oppression have generated trauma in ourselves and our communities. These are not mutually exclusive domains of study and I think we need people working on all levels. But at this moment, when "trauma-informed care" is a true craze in mental health treatment, it seems less common to consider how trauma is generated by racism, sexism, xenophobia, and the other endless forms of intolerance. To me, this is one of the truly unique and exciting things about this play: that even while presenting an intensely personal story of three women, the characters' own histories so deftly invoke the whole landscape of what we call trauma.

Erin, what a joy and an honor to be asked to talk about this fantastic and moving play. When you started this conversation between us, you asked about rules and assumptions. As someone who knows so little about dramaturgy, but who is curious about your own creative process, I am wondering about how you thought about the "rules" as you were writing this. Were there any rules you set out to break? More specifically, did you think about how much you wanted to faithfully reproduce certain elements of the science, versus break those rules and create your own version of it? What expectations and assumptions did you confront in your own process, and how did you think about the expectations an audience member might bring to a work like this?

Erin Courtney: I went back and forth on how much science to put in the play and how much to fictionalize the science. I am so grateful that you invited me to share my play with your science/writing group Neuwrite and one of my favorite comments from the group was that I put too much science in that draft I shared. I'm paraphrasing but they said something to the effect of "more theater, less science!" So that was a gift and it reminded me that I am writing a play! The initial inspiration for the play came from an interview on NPR about Persinger's "God Helmet." I was delighted to hear that people with religious practices felt/saw God or had a spiritual feeling when wearing the helmet and that atheists and agnostics sometimes saw supernatural things like TROLLS IN FORESTS, which is not what I was expecting to hear. So I was determined to write a play that featured the God Helmet. When I later read about Capgras Syndrome, the syndrome in which your brain does not recognize a loved one and you are certain they have been replaced by an imposter, I knew that the other neuroscientist in the play would be studying that.

Then I set about making some rules for myself: the play would be three women, the play would take place in one physical location (which is not how I usually situate plays), the play would somehow utilize the symmetry and reflection as seen in tile design, the play would be about neuroscience. During one of the Space on Ryder Farm residencies, I made a very exciting rule/organizing structure that the play would consist of four scenes with each scene reflecting and rotating the point of view, a sort of replay of the same event from different angles. With great enthusiasm I tried this approach but when I shared my pages, I hated them. They sounded dead. I was so upset and Ethan Lipton, who was also in residence at the farm, asked me, "Well what did you do differently than what you usually do?" I said "I wrote from an outline and it sounds dead." Ethan said, "Well then, stop writing from an outline." I began writing the play again without an outline and instead of having whole scenes repeat from a different angle, I chose to have smaller bites of language repeat and rotate. So sometimes I create a series of rules that turn out to be the wrong rules and then have to throw those out and make a new set of rules.

The topic of assumptions is a big one for me, in terms of form and content. Formally, American playwrights have a sort of default subconscious setting that theater must be constructed as naturalistic, linear, and focused on one protagonist. We shouldn't assume that every story/experience will be served by that structure. In terms of content, so much violence and cruelty comes from making false assumptions. In researching how the brain works, it turns out our brains are constantly filling in blind spots with information pulled from what we already know—it's a necessary shortcut. Well, the only way around it is to learn, see, experience more so that when our brains make the shortcut, we have more data to pull from.

The question of expectations of audience members is also super interesting. A lot of playwrights and theater makers I know talk about how a play teaches the audience how to watch it, especially if you are utilizing a non-traditional tone, structure, or content. In this play, the mirror exercise, the married couple repeating each other's language, lets us know this play will be about repetition. Sarah Lunnie at one point suggested that I utilize that mirror exercise again in the play and once I did that I could see audiences enjoyed the familiarity of the return of that exchange and it helped them stay inside the play.

I'm glad that both Carl and José spoke about messiness and faith. Sometimes my obsession with pattern can leave little room for formal messiness, but my hope is the character's emotional complexity remains somewhat unruly, and the human connection to mystery allows space for further exploration in art, science, love, and recovery.

acknowledgments

Thank you to Adam Greenfield, Tim Sanford, and Sarah Lunnie at Playwrights Horizons for commissioning and developing this play. The radical generosity of the staff and artists of the Working Farm Residency at Space on Ryder Farm, specifically the vision and hard work of Emily Simoness and John Baker, helped the play find its form and voice. Thank you to Hayley Finn and Jeremy Cohen for the gift of developing the play at the Playwrights' Center in Minneapolis; to Maria Striar and the playwrights of Clubbed Thumb Writers Group; to Kate Kremer and Jess Barbagallo of 53rd State Press; to Carl Erik Fisher, M.D. and Neuwrite, Columbia University's science writing collective; to Madeleine Oldham and The Ground Floor at Berkeley Rep; to Emily Morse and the New Dramatists community; to my agent, Michael Finkle at WME; and to Mac Wellman and all the playwrights that continue to inspire me from the Brooklyn College family. Many thanks to Taibi Magar and José Zayas, who have directed the play with intelligence and care. Endless gratitude to the following brilliant actors who workshopped the play along the way: Marinda Anderson, Christina Baldwin, Zabryna Guevarra, Zuleyma Guevarra, Birgit Huppuch, Rachel Leslie, April Matthis, Kelly McAndrew, Nora Montañez Patterson, Thomasina Petrus, Miriam Silverman, Heather Alicia Simms, and Carmen Zilles. My personal gratitude to Gretchen Grace, Shawn Chen, Lila Neugebauer, and Heidi Schreck. Finally, ongoing thanks and deep love to my husband, Scott Adkins; my sons, Charlie and Theo; my siblings, Colleen Cole, Jake Courtney, and Mary Burke; and my parents, Bob and Dorothy Courtney.

contributors

Erin Courtney is an award-winning, New York-based playwright. Her play, *A Map of Virtue*, produced by 13P and directed by Ken Rus Schmoll, was awarded an Obie and described as "one of the most terrifying plays of the past decade" by Alexis Soloski in The New York Times. *A Map of Virtue* was nominated for a GLAAD Media Award for Outstanding New York Theater, and has had numerous productions across the country. Her play *I Will Be Gone*, directed by Kip Fagan, premiered at the Humana Festival, Actors Theater of Louisville in 2015. She has written two operas with Elizabeth Swados: *The Nomad* and *Kaspar Hauser*. The musical, *The Tattooed Lady*, which she is writing with composer and lyricist Max Vernon, has been developed with support from The Rhinebeck Writer's Retreat, The Kimmel Center, and Joe's Pub at The Public Theater. Her other plays, produced by Clubbed Thumb, include *Alice The Magnet*, directed by Pam MacKinnon, and *Demon Baby*, directed by Ken Rus Schmoll. She is an affiliated artist with Clubbed Thumb, a member of the Obie Award-winning playwright's collective 13P, as well as the co-founder of the Brooklyn Writers Space. Ms. Courtney taught playwriting at the MFA program at Brooklyn College for fifteen years and is now an Assistant Professor in the Radio, Television, and Film Department at Northwestern University. She is an alumnus of New Dramatists, a MacDowell Colony Fellow, a Core Writer at the Playwrights' Center, and a member of The Working Farm at Space on Ryder Farm. She was awarded a Guggenheim Fellowship in 2013.

Carl Erik Fisher, M.D. is an Assistant Professor of Clinical Psychiatry at Columbia University, where he also teaches in the Masters in Bioethics program. He studies law, ethics, and policy relating to psychiatry and neuroscience, with a particular focus on substance use disorders and other addictive behaviors.His writing has been published in JAMA, The American Journal of Bioethics, and The Journal of Medical Ethics, among others. He has written for the public in Slate and Scientific American MIND, and he is currently writing a book-length intellectual and cultural history of addiction, The War Within (Penguin Press, Summer 2021).

Sarah Lunnie is a dramaturg who works, primarily, on new plays. Recent production collaborations include Anne Washburn's *Shipwreck*; Heidi Schreck's *What The Constitution Means to Me*; Lucas Hnath's *A Doll's House, Part 2*, *Hillary and Clinton*, and *The Thin Place*; The Mad Ones' *Miles for Mary* and *Mrs. Murray's Menagerie*; and Jeff Augustin and the Bengsons' *Where The Mountain Meets The Sea*, which played to one audience before the coronavirus pandemic shuttered the American theater. Sarah has been an associate artistic director of the Jungle Theater in Minneapolis, the literary director at Playwrights

Horizons, and the literary manager at Actors Theatre of Louisville. She is a company member of The Mad Ones and makes audio plays for very small audiences with Telephonic Literary Union. She lives with her family in Brooklyn.

José Zayas has directed over 100 productions in New York, regionally, and internationally. He has premiered works by Hilary Bettis, Nilo Cruz, Caridad Svich, Robert Askins, Thomas Bradshaw, Duncan Sheik, Steven Sater, Stephin Merritt, Taylor Mac, Susan Kim, Andrea Thome, Lynn Rosen, Saviana Stanescu, Carlos Murillo, Rob Urbinati, Kristina Poe, Catherine Filloux, James Carter, Matt Barbot, Paco Gamez and Jordi Galceran. José is a Drama League Fellow and is associated with Lincoln Center's Director's Lab, SoHo Rep Writers/Director's Lab, and the NEA/TCG Career Development Program for Directors. He is an Ensemble Studio Theatre member, a Resident Director at Repertorio Español 2009-2019, a Lortel Nominating Committee member, and curator of Two River Theater's Crossing Borders Festival. BA: Harvard University. MFA: Carnegie Mellon. josezayasdirector.com.

also from 53rd state press

The Book of the Dog // Karinne Keithley
Joyce Cho Plays // Joyce Cho
No Dice // Nature Theater of Oklahoma
When You Rise Up // Miguel Gutierrez
Montgomery Park, or Opulence // Karinne Keithley
Crime or Emergency // Sibyl Kempson
Off the Hozzle // Rob Erickson
A Map of Virtue + Black Cat Lost // Erin Courtney
Pig Iron: Three Plays // Pig Iron Theatre Company
The Mayor of Baltimore + Anthem // Kristen Kosmas
Ich, Kürbisgeist + The Secret Death of Puppets // Sibyl Kempson
Soulographie: Our Genocides // Erik Ehn
Life and Times: Episode 1 // Nature Theater of Oklahoma
Life and Times: Episode 2 // Nature Theater of Oklahoma
Life and Times: Episode 3 + 4 // Nature Theater of Oklahoma
The 53rd State Occasional No. 1 // Ed. Paul Lazar
There There // Kristen Kosmas
Seagull (Thinking of You) // Tina Satter
Self Made Man Man Made Land // Ursula Eagly
Another Telepathic Thing // Big Dance Theater
Another Tree Dance // Karinne Keithley Syers
Let Us Now Praise Susan Sontag // Sibyl Kempson
Dance by Letter // Annie-B Parson
Pop Star Series // Neal Medlyn
The Javier Plays // Carlos Murillo
Minor Theater: Three Plays // Julia Jarcho
Ghost Rings (12-inch vinyl) // Half Straddle
A New Practical Guide to Rhetorical Gesture and Action // NTUSA
A Field Guide to iLANDing // iLAND
The 53rd State Occasional No. 2 // Ed. Will Arbery
Suicide Forest // Haruna Lee
Rude Mechs' Lipstick Traces // Lana Lesley + the Rude Mechs
MILTON // PearlDamour
The People's Republic of Valerie, Living Room Edition // Kristen Kosmas

Uncollected Trash Collection // Kate Kremer
A Discourse on Method // David Levine + Shonni Enelow
Severed // Ignacio Lopez
Ann, Fran, and Mary Ann // Erin Courtney

FORTHCOMING
I Understand Everything Better // David Neumann + Sibyl Kempson
ASTRS // Karinne Keithley Syers
Love Like Light // Daniel Alexander Jones
SKiNFoLK: An American Show // Jillian Walker
Wood Calls Out to Wood // Corinne Donly
Karen Davis: Bitter Pill, Mistook Acerbic for Advil // Jess Barbagallo
WATER SPORTS; or insignificant white boys // Jeremy O. Harris
12 Shouts to the Ten Forgotten Heavens: Springs // Sibyl Kempson
Broken Clothing // Suzanne Bocanegra

Book design: Kate Kremer
Cover & interior images: Erin Courtney
Cover design: vind datter

53rd State Press publishes lucid, challenging, and lively new writing for performance. Our catalog includes new plays as well as scores and notations for interdisciplinary performance, graphic adaptations, and essays on theater and dance.

53rd State Press was founded in 2007 by Karinne Keithley in response to the bounty of new writing in the downtown New York community that was not available except in the occasional reading or short-lived performance. In 2010, Antje Oegel joined her as a co-editor. In 2017, Kate Kremer took on the leadership of the volunteer editorial collective.

For more information or to order books, please visit 53rdstatepress.org.

53rd State Press books are represented to the trade by TCG (Theatre Communications Group). TCG books are exclusively distributed to the book trade by Consortium Book Sales and Distribution, an Ingram Brand.

Ann, Fran, and Mary Ann is made possible by the New York State Council on the Arts with the support of Governor Andrew M. Cuomo and the New York State Legislature.

53rd State Press
new writing for performance